All About

Leaves

Claire Throp

capstone

Edited by Claire Throp and Brynn Baker
Designed by Peggie Carley
Picture research by Ruth Blair
Production by Victoria Fitzgerald
Originated by Capstone Global Library Ltd

**Library of Congress Cataloging-in-Publication
Data**

ISBN 978-1-4846-0507-3 (hardcover)
ISBN 978-1-4846-3847-7 (paperback)
ISBN 978-1-4846-0513-4 (ebook PDF)

Acknowledgments
We would like to thank the following for
permission to reproduce photographs:
Dreamstime: Egon Zitter, 7, Mommamoon, 16,
Erin Packard Photography, 21; iStock: Tedy2g, 12;
Shutterstock: Barry Blackburn, 14, Bobkeenan
Photography, 17, byggarn.se, 18, Chris Bence,
20, DenisNata, 9, 23 (middle), Elena Elisseeva, 4,
Filipe B. Varela, 5, Nataliya Hora, 10, Pefkos, cover,
Photobac, 22, pixelman, 13, 23 (bottom), Smileus,
6, 11, Songquan Deng, back cover, 19, 23 (top),
Suphatthra China, 15, Triff, 8

We would like to thank Michael Bright for his
invaluable help in the preparation of this book.

Every effort has been made to contact copyright
holders of material reproduced in this book.
Any omissions will be rectified in subsequent
printings if notice is given to the publisher.

Contents

What Are Plants?

Plants are living things.

flower

stem

leaf

root

seed

Plants have
many parts.

What Do Plants Need to Grow?

Plants need sunlight and air to grow.

Plants need water to grow.

What Are Leaves?

A leaf is one part of a plant.

Leaves grow from a plant's **stem**.

Leaves make food for the plant.

Leaves use sunlight to make the food.

Types of Leaves

There are different types of leaves. Some leaves are long and thin.

Some leaves have **wavy** edges.

Some plants have very big leaves.

Some plants have very
small leaves.

Colors

Most leaves are green.

Some leaves stay green all year.

Some leaves turn red in the fall.

Other leaves turn yellow, orange, or brown in the fall.

Leaves as Food

Some animals like to eat leaves.

Some insects like to eat leaves too.

Plants Need Leaves

Leaves make food to help a
plant grow.

Picture Glossary

 **fall** season when leaves turn red, yellow, orange, and brown

 **stem** strong part of a plant that holds up the leaves

 **wavy** many curves in a line

Index

Notes for Parents and Teachers

Before Reading

Gather together a variety of leaves or photos of leaves. If it is not fall, find photos of leaves before and after they have changed color. Ask children why they think some leaves change color and some do not. Talk about how some leaves change during different seasons.

After Reading

- Ask children why leaves are so important for plants. (They make food.)

- If possible, take children outside and see if they can find a selection of different shaped leaves. Then use books or the internet to figure out the type of plants or trees.

- Work with children to capture ideas about leaves, such as descriptions of their colors, why leaves are useful, and so on. Have them use vivid adjectives and precise verbs, such as *scarlet shapes against the limbs* or *food and shelter for other living things.* After children have contributed phrases, work as a class to combine those phrases to create a poem. Children may add illustrations or photos to the class poem.